Contents

Overview

Authority

The DOI Social Media Guidebook is published under the authority of 110 DM 5.3 D, of the Departmental Manual.

Purpose

The DOI Social Media Guidebook provides official guidance to bureaus and offices in their use of social media and related tools, including but not limited to:

Website-embedded Services (not limited to analytics and widgets, including "share" buttons)

Social Networking Sites

Blogs and Microblogs

Comments to DOI Posts

Document- and Data-sharing Repositories

Social Bookmarking Services

Some elements of the guidebook are hard rules. Others are recommendations. Still others are requests for advice. As with most SocMed use, collaboration will generally be more helpful than criticism.

The associated DOI Social Media Policy outlines specific rules for the use of social media at DOI. Before embarking on any use of social media for official purposes, consult the Social Media Policy.

This is a living (official) document, undergoing edits on a frequent basis. It is not recommended that you print this guidebook; rather, please work from the current online edition.

Website-embedded Services

Requirements

DOI websites (e.g. DOI.gov) may use third-party embedded code, provided that certain procedures are followed:

A. Embedded code must be evaluated by IT security to ensure it does not introduce vulnerabilities into any DOI site. Consult with IT security officials in your bureau before embedding code on your site.

B. DOI or bureau websites employing embedded code must disclaim endorsement for the code and/or the code's provider, or the suitability of the code for any other use. The site must also disclaim that any non-Federal external site linked to the code is outside of DOI or bureau control. Neither DOI, nor the bureau, take responsibility for the external site's compliance, or lack thereof, with any law, regulation, or DOI or bureau policy. Terms of Service (TOS): DOI must have approved Terms of Service with the provider. Generally, TOS negotiation occurs at the DOI/OCO level, so the revised/amended TOS may apply to all DOI bureaus and offices. Bureaus and offices should not conduct their own TOS negotiations for such services without permission of OCO, to avoid replication of efforts.

C. Privacy Impact Assessment (PIA): DOI requires a preliminary PIA for all systems. The preliminary PIA determines if the system contains PII, and is kept as a record by the Department. The PIA documents the assessment of how government actions may affect citizens, providing both a paper trail and an opportunity for multiple parties to offer thoughts, criticism and approval or disapproval. Contact your privacy officer for further information on Privacy Impact Assessments.

D. System of Records Notice (SORN): Any DOI action which creates a System of Records may only create it within the auspices of a System of Records Notice.

E. Failure to comply: Failure to comply with the above may result in disciplinary action. Creation of a System of Records without a proper SORN may result in fines ranging from $1000 to $5000.

F. With rare exceptions, we do not approve of embedded code which provides identity data of our website users to third parties. For example, social media buttons and embeddable feeds of various forms can typically transmit identity information and plant cookies. Such buttons and feeds should not be used.

Types of Services

Analytics (Google Analytics)

According to DOI's PIA, any IP address passed from our users to the analytics provider will have its final octet masked to allow limited geolocation-based reporting but will both prevent the IP address from being considered PII and deal with certain privacy concerns.

"Share" buttons ~~(AddThis)~~

NOTE: OS No longer uses AddThis. Our replacement code "NCShare" (No Cookie Share) is available on GitHub (https://github.com/usinterior/ncshare).

~~DOI has approved the AddThis social media "share" button service. This does not imply any endorsement of AddThis, merely that TOS and PIA have been completed for this service.~~

a. ~~When creating an AddThis "share" button, you may activate analytics. AddThis analytics do not provide DOI with PII.~~

b. No other "share" buttons have been approved.

   i. Note: Certain popular SocMed "share" tools have been noted in the popular press for their data-gathering technology.

   ii. The DOI New Media team is particularly wary of placing externally sourced code on .gov websites (and any other sites that we might have authority over) that runs a risk of degrading user privacy.

Video (YouTube)

DOI has approved YouTube embedding, under certain conditions. Please see "Appendix A – Additional Guidance for Approved services" for details.

Document sharing (SlideShare)

DOI has approved SlideShare embedding, under certain conditions. Please see "Appendix A – Additional Guidance for Approved services" for details.

Widgets and other embedded code

A widget is a portable piece of computer code that can be executed within a Web page to allow content from one site to be presented dynamically within another. Widgets often take the form of on-screen tools (clocks, event countdowns, auction tickers, stock market tickers, flight arrival information, daily weather, etc).

At present, limited "widget" code has been approved for use. Please see the individual entries for various services in this Guidebook, as well as Requirements F (above).

TOS/PIA Updates

Consult with your bureau's social media contact for the latest list of signed terms of service agreements and PIAs.

Social Networking Sites

Social networks connect people, often those who share the same interests and/or activities or who are interested in exploring the interests and activities of others. Interagency and intergovernmental social networking sites can promote cooperation across government. Internal social networking sites can establish connections across traditionally stove-piped and geographically dispersed organizations. Public social networking sites can be used to further promote government information and services. By setting up a group in Facebook, for example, government can provide information resources and staff interaction with members of the public who are interested in a facet of an agency's work and mission. Doing so expands the government's outreach capabilities and ability to interact.

1. Rules of the Road

    A. The DOI Social Media Policy addresses specific guidelines for the appropriate use of social networking websites and other social media technologies. Consult the policy before getting started

    B. Only post information that is publicly available on the primary bureau or Departmental website (OMB M-10-23, Section 3, "Agencies should also provide individuals with alternatives to third-party websites and applications. People should be able to obtain comparable information and services through an agency's official website or other official means.").

C. Social networking sites generally allow for comments to be submitted in response to posts. Refer to the Social Media Comments section, below.

D. Work with your bureau records management office to determine how content posted on social networking sites and the comments submitted as responses should be managed as Federal records. See Social Media Records Retention.

E. Follow the applicable rules pertaining to the revelation of personally identifiable information (PII) of DOI employees via social networking sites.

F. Be sure that commercial advertising does not appear on your social media site, prior to making the site public, whenever possible.

G. Do not engage in arguments or debates. Social networking websites are not the place to engage in debates over policy with members of the public or interest groups. Responding factually to substantive questions is OK, but engaging in policy debate is not. See the Response to Social Media Comments flowchart in Appendix B.

H. TOS, Privacy, SORN

1) Do not use a service in a manner that would violate DOI's TOS, PIA or social media System of Records Notice.

2) Consult with your bureau's social media contact for the latest list of signed terms of service agreements and PIA's.

2. Examples of Government Use

A. Facebook: White House: http://www.facebook.com/whitehouse

B. Facebook: State Department: http://www.facebook.com/pages/Washington-DC/US-Department-of-State/15877306073

C. YouTube: White House: http://www.youtube.com/user/whitehouse

Blogging and Microblogging

There are many benefits and risks in maintaining a public blog on a Government website, with the top risk being the potential legal liabilities. Although blogs are generally meant to be informal, DOI blogs are official Government communications and must be treated as such. Their content must be controlled to ensure that it is in keeping with the mission and reputation of the authoring agency.

Microblogs consist of short entries (usually 140 characters or fewer) and are generally posted through third-party sites such as Twitter.

1. Rules of the Road

A. First, consult the DOI Social Media Policy.

B. Blog Approval and Management

- All blogs hosted on Department of the Interior owned or sponsored public websites must be approved by the bureau's office of communications or public affairs prior to creation and implementation of the blog. The office of communications or public affairs will help determine if other entities within the bureau or Department must be notified or consulted about the blog prior to creation. Such entities might include, but are not limited to, the Office of the Chief Information Officer, the Office of the Solicitor, or records and privacy officials.

- Blog topics must both avoid areas of potential litigation and the appearance of being an official channel for comments used as part of a rulemaking process.

- Blog posts must be written by Interior personnel. Per SOL memorandum "External Author Blog" dated September 19, 2011, "Allowing an author outside the Department of the Interior (DOI) to blog … presents problems including noncompliance with information quality guidelines pursuant to the Information Quality Act and the possible appearance of endorsement by DOI of specific organizations or companies."

- Prior to implementation of the blog, bureaus and offices must notify the appropriate personnel in the Departmental Office of the Chief Information Officer (OCIO) and Departmental Office of Communications (OCO) of all approved bureau or office blogs and provide the following information: the purpose of the blog; proposed blog Web address (URL); and point of contact information. Failure to obtain required approvals or to make required notifications prior to implementation may result in removal of the blog from the hosting website.

C. Approval and creation of a new blog requires that DOI bureaus or offices

- Examine the need for the blog style and justify why a standard information feed would not be sufficient.

- Have a policy in place that governs who can post a blog.

- Identify the DOI bureau/office author on the blog;

- Establish a procedure for reviewing/approving blog entries;

- Establish a process for archiving the information on the blog and retaining blog content according to its records disposition schedule (See Appendix E);

- Establish a policy regarding editing/disqualifying submissions if the public is allowed to place comments on the blog;

- Establish a policy regarding replies to comments or questions if the public is allowed to submit blog comments;

- Include privacy, FOIA, and disclaimer notices on the site, as appropriate; and

- Address all IT security concerns associated with the blogging software and its use on Government Web servers.

2. Blog Content

   A. Anything posted to the Web that is managed, maintained, hosted, or sponsored by the Department of the Interior and/or any of its offices or bureaus is an official government publication and must comply with all applicable Federal laws and policies and the DOI Web Standards.

   B. As an official publication of a U.S. Government organization, blogs must be fair, accurate, and as unbiased as possible while supporting the DOI mission. Blogging activities must not interfere with the agency's primary mission.

   C. Blogs are intended for the informal exchange of information and ideas and not as a conduit to receive official comments on bureau proposed rule-making. They play no official role in organizational decision-making. Citizens wishing to leave comments regarding Federal Register notices must do so via the process described in the notice.

   D. Blogs must be predictable, reliable, and dependable. Once a blog is started, it must be regularly updated. On occasion, blogs may be established to support a specific project or study. When the project of study is completed, the last blog entry will clearly indicate the date blog entries were ended.

   E. Blog content provided by DOI or bureau representatives must meet the accepted DOI or Bureau standards for information quality. DOI and bureaus must have a process in place for ensuring that content meets DOI or bureau standards. Links from blogs must comply with Departmental linking policies in the DOI Web Standards, (3.4 Linking Policies and Linking to Non-Federal websites).

Web/Social Media Comments

Comments received through two-way blogs must be reviewed by the bureau (or DOI if it is a Departmental blog). Each blog must have clear and defensible standards for comments. All sites that allow visitors to post comments should make it clear whether comments will be moderated and should include a disclaimer. For example:

"We welcome your comments and hope that our conversations here will be courteous. You are fully responsible for the content of your comments.

"We do not discriminate against any views, but we reserve the right to delete any of the following:

- off-topic comments

- violent, vulgar, obscene, profane, hateful, or racist comments

- comments that threaten or defame any person or organization

- The violation of the privacy of another individual

- solicitations, advertisements, or endorsements of any financial, commercial, or non-governmental agency

- comments that suggest or encourage illegal activity

- comments promoting or opposing any person who is campaigning for election to a political office or promoting or opposing any ballot proposition

- comments including phone numbers, e-mail addresses, residential addresses, or similar information

- multiple, successive off-topic posts by a single user

- repetitive posts copied and pasted by multiple users"

"Communication made through this service's e-mail and/or messaging system will in no way constitute a legal or official notice or comment to the U.S. Department of the Interior (or bureau) or any official or employee of the U.S. Department of the Interior (or bureau) for any purpose.

"References to commercial entities, products, services, or nongovernmental organizations or individuals are provided solely for information. These references are not intended to reflect the opinion of U.S. Department of the Interior (or bureau), the United States Government, or its officers or employees concerning the significance, priority, or importance to be given the referenced entity, product, service, or organization. Such references are not an official or personal endorsement of any product, person, or service and may not be quoted or reproduced for the purpose of stating or implying U.S. Department of the Interior (or bureau) endorsement or approval of any product, person, or service.

"Reporters or other media representatives are asked to send questions through their normal channels (the appropriate DOI/bureau office public affairs or communications office) and to refrain from submitting questions here as comments. Reporter questions may be removed.

"This Comment Policy is subject to amendment or modification at any time to ensure that its continued use is consistent with its intended purpose as a limited forum."

Document- and Data-Sharing Repositories

Document and data sharing websites are just what their name implies: places where users post information and material that other users can use and repurpose, creating a dynamic repository covering a potentially wide variety of subjects. Data.gov is one example of a government repository for information, but there are many other established online sites in the commercial sector that can also be used to make data and information available to the public and for the public to provide the government with valuable information. Document sharing websites (e.g., Scribd, SlideShare, and Socrata) can share documents, presentations, webinars, and/or datasets with the public.

At present, SlideShare has been approved by DOI; however, this should not be taken as an endorsement of SlideShare, nor an indication that other document-sharing websites will not be approved.

1. Rules of the Road

A. The DOI Social Media Policy addresses specific guidelines for the appropriate use of Document Sharing websites and other social media technologies. Consult the policy before getting started. An additional link to the Social Media Policy may be found in the footer of DOI.gov.

B. Only post information that is ready for public consumption and has been approved through regular review processes. Never post data or information that is only for internal view or use to a public website. This is not the place to post or share working documents. Although most services protect accounts via passwords, stored files are not necessarily encrypted, so a successful hacker might gain access to stored-but-unpublished files on such a service.

C. External (non-.gov) document repository websites should never be the only source of a DOI document available to the public. All documents posted on document repository websites should also be publicly available on a bureau or office website.

D. Privacy & SORN

   1) Use document-sharing sites only in a manner consistent with DOI's approved PIA.

   2) Under no circumstances should anyone use a document-sharing site in such a way as to violate DOI's social media System of Records Notice. Establishing a system of records in violation of a system of records notice may result in large fines and disciplinary action.

E. Please see "Appendix A – Additional Guidance for Approved services" for further details.

2. Examples of Government Use

   A. DOI OCO: http://www.doi.gov/news/pressreleases/AMERICAS-GREAT-OUTDOORS-Salazar-Releases-50-State-Report-Highlighting-Projects-to-Promote-Conservation-Outdoor-Recreation.cfm. OCO uses SlideShare as a document-embedding tool more than as a centralized document repository. Your use may vary.

   B. EPA (Scribd): http://www.scribd.com/doc/13232289/Blogging-At-EPA-Guidelines

   C. White House (Socrata): http://www.whitehouse.gov/blog/Annual-Report-to-Congress-on-White-House-Staff-2009/

Social Bookmarking

Social bookmarking tools like Digg, Reddit, or Delicious allow users to share links to interesting information with larger audiences. These Web services typically allow users to organize their bookmarks using tags and share them either with the public, a specified group, or privately. Adding a simple widget on DOI or bureau content pages that allows visitors to share the content of the page via social bookmarking tools, social networking tools, or e-mail is a simple way that DOI and bureaus can drive traffic to their websites and allow visitors to quickly and easily share our information with their networks or communities.

At present, *no such site is approved for use by DOI*; however, in anticipation of future approvals, the following will apply:

1. Rules of the Road

   o The DOI Social Media Policy addresses specific guidelines for the appropriate use of social bookmarking Web services and other social media technologies. Consult the policy before beginning any implementation.

   o TOS, Privacy, SORN

      ▪ Only use services that have an approved TOS and privacy impact assessment signed by the Department of the Interior.

      ▪ Be sure that any "sharing" on public-facing Web space does not point to non-public content. The URL might be helpful to hackers.

      ▪ Do not use a service in a manner that would violate DOI's social media System of Records Notice. Establishing a system of records in violation of a system of records notice may result in large fines and disciplinary action.

      ▪ Consult with your bureau's social media contact for the latest list of signed terms of service agreements and PIA's.

2. Examples of Government Use

   o DHS: Share This Page: http://www.dhs.gov/index.shtm

   o State Department: Bookmark: http://www.state.gov/

   o USA.gov: Share: http://www.usa.gov/

Appendix A – Additional Guidance for Approved services

Requirements

1. Remember the TOS/PIA/SORN.

   - **TOS** – DOI must approve terms of service with the provider. GSA approval is not enough.

   - **PIA** – DOI requires an approved Privacy Impact Assessment (or preliminary PIA).

   - **SORN** – Any social media use which would create or make use of a system of records must be used only within the boundaries of a published System of Records Notice.

2. For any service that sends IP addresses to the provider, mask the final octet of all IP addresses whenever practical. DOI considers a full IP address as PII. Masking the final octet simplifies privacy issues by negating its PII status.

3. Request approval from your bureau's social media contact.

4. Contact DOI (via GSA's Apps.gov portal, if possible) for all account approvals for services listed in this appendix. One contact person has been assigned responsibility for account management as per negotiation with service providers.

5. When registering for services

   a. Use an office e-mail address, rather than a personal address. For example, OCO generally uses newmedia@ios.doi.gov. Using a personal account (i.e. Bob_Smith@ios.doi.gov) can lead to complications when the account holder leaves DOI.

   b. Be sure that either 1) more than one person has the account name and password for all services or 2) more than one administrative account (with one person for each account) is set up for each service.

   c. If the account registration process requires a birth date, please use March 3, 1949 (the centennial anniversary of DOI) for consistency. March 3, 1849 is generally unavailable.

   d. Click through the normal TOS, but notify the DOI OCO Social Media Contact to be added to the "official" list of DOI users, so we can respond properly to OPM and Congressional inquiries and maintain our master list of social media accounts.

Services

AddThis

DOI's Digital Strategy Team no longer uses AddThis. Instead, we use NCShare (No Cookie Share), which is available on our GitHub account: https://github.com/usinterior/ncshare

If your office uses AddThis analytics, it is possible (and approved) to use AddThis links in your Tweets, to enhance the breadth of the tool's reach. On the other hand, it's also possible (and

~~approved) to maintain separate links, in order to separately analyze Web and Twitter outreach. Please feel free to share your results as you work with the service and test its capabilities. No "best practice" has been determined on this matter, yet.~~

~~For those of us using both Google Analytics and AddThis, there is a customization available, to allow monitoring of AddThis analytics from your GA dashboard, putting both analytics in one place for easy viewing: http://www.addthis.com/help/google-analytics-integration. We're experimenting with it on DOI.gov and will let you know how it goes.~~

Bit.ly

1. Bit.ly is the default URL shortener for .gov URLs.

2. The GSA arrangement with Bit.ly allows for default shortening of .gov addresses to the form 1.usa.gov/######.

3. DOI's Digital Strategy team has arranged for shortened URL's in the form on.DOI.gov/###### for all DOI URLs. We also have access to Bit.ly's API.

4. Bureaus and offices which would like to use on.DOI.gov short-URLs should contact DOI's New Media Team. At present, DOI.gov, BLM.gov, USBR.gov, and USGS.gov URLs all automatically shorten to on.DOI.gov URLs in Bit.ly.

5. Do not build a custom URL-shortener. DOI would like to avoid creating a multi-year support/dependence situation to solve a problem (URL shortening) that has already been solved.

Challenge.gov

- Establish clear and descriptive rules for who is eligible to win a prize. Include information about minimum age, who's eligible (e.g., public, Feds, contractors), U.S. Citizens, etc

- Address how intellectual property and copyrights will be handled for any products that will be submitted, or created from submissions, by DOI or the bureau. Be sure to also address any privacy and liability concerns with the use by the Government of the items being submitted.

- Ensure that products being submitted for the challenge meet 508 requirements for government products.

- Provide clear instructions on how to submit entires, how entries will be judged and timeframes/deadlines for entries.

- Clearly state the exact prizes that are available, how monetary prizes will be distributed, and other specifics on how prizes will be managed

- GSA has not provided a SORN for Challenge.gov, so be certain that your information-gathering falls under the DOI Social Media SORN. Regarding "additional information" gathered by agencies that use Challenge.gov, GSA's PIA reads as follows (emphasis added):

If this includes any PII, it will be the responsibility of the agency sponsoring the challenge to ensure that the privacy of that information is protected. (Challenge.gov PIA, page 4, Solving a Challenge)

crowdSPRING

Please do not use crowdSPRING without first consulting with DOI's New Media team.

Facebook

1. When possible, obtain a custom URL for your official page(s). Default Facebook URLs are long and unwieldy.

2. When adding video to Facebook, don't forget to add captioning. At the time of this writing, Facebook uses SRT timed-text files: https://www.facebook.com/help/www/261764017354370

3. Maintain vigilance for "rogue" or "community" pages (see Facebook Community Pages, below) that appear to be official pages. Contact your bureau's social media contact to have them purged.

4. From Facebook [some emphases, formatting and additional text added]:

   To create a new Facebook Government Page [only after receiving approval from your bureau social media contact]:

   - Go to http://www.Facebook.com/page.

   - Select "Brand, Product, or Organization" and create a "Government" page.

   - When you agree to create a page, the signed [government TOS] agreement with Facebook supersedes the site's terms.

   - As you create the page, you can choose "Do not make Page publicly visible at this time." You will be able to edit and publish later.

   - Once you've created a page, it remains unpublished (not visible to the public) until you choose to publish it.

   - Setup the page and add content.

   - Please remember the federal agreement requires you to include this language on the page *"If you're looking for the official source of information about [Government Entity], please visit our homepage at [URL Link]."*

   - Notify your bureau social media contact, who should refer up the chain to the Director of Digital Strategy. The director (or assignee) will email the page URL to USgovernment@facebook.com and request that ads be removed. Please do not contact USgovernment@facebook.com at a lower level than the bureau social media contact for any reason, without first clearing that contact with your bureau social media contact.

   - Facebook will respond once this request has been processed.

Existing Pages

- Notify your bureau social media contact, who should refer up the chain to the Director of Digital Strategy. The director (or assignee) will email the page URL to USgovernment@facebook.com and request that ads be removed. Please do not contact USgovernment@facebook.com at a lower level than the bureau social media contact for any reason, without first clearing that contact with your bureau social media contact.

- Facebook will respond once this request has been processed.

Additional Tips for Managing Your Page:

- Read the Facebook Pages help section (http://www.facebook.com/help/#/help/?page=175).

- You can access all of the pages you admin by going to http://www.facebook.com/pages/manage.

- Please be aware that in order to create a Facebook Page, you must have a Facebook Profile. A Facebook Page is administered by a Facebook Personal Profile account for security reasons. That account can then add other Facebook users as administrators to help maintain the Page. Admins are not public and thus are not visible to other Facebook users. More information on page admins is available here in our help section (http://www.facebook.com/help/#/help.php?page=904)

- Be sure to add several administrators to the page (http://www.facebook.com/help/#/help/?faq=15188).

For resources on how best to utilize Facebook, please refer visit our 'Help' page (http://www.facebook.com/help.php). You'll find lots of information about Facebook as well as many answers to your questions.

Additional resources can be found in the Facebook Help Section (http://www.facebook.com/help), The Facebook and Government Page (http://www.facebook.com/government), and on the Facebook Pages page (http://www.facebook.com/FacebookPages). Please note that this email address should not be contacted for general questions about the site, please refer to the Facebook Help Section (http://www.facebook.com/help).

Facebook Community Pages (A.K.A. "Fake" Facebook pages)

1. Facebook's bots roam through public postings collecting content. When their system detects subjects of online conversation (for example, "DOI" or "Bureau of Land Management") it creates a "Community Page" about that subject. It generally pulls descriptive text and an image from Wikipedia and the aforementioned comments from Facebook. It then continues to populate the "wall" with updated comments from Facebook. The result is a page that looks like an official page (complete with Facebook "likes"), but isn't.

2. Don't blame Wikipedia. Much of the content in Facebook's "Community pages" comes from Wikipedia, occasionally leading to the mistaken belief that Wikipedia is part of the "Community Page" situation. Those pages are created by Facebook and copy content from Wikipedia.

3. Facebook has sent instructions for dealing with this issue: "Review our IP reporting procedures at http://www.facebook.com/legal/copyright.php?howto_report and use the link to our 'automated IP infringement form.' If you are a government entity, please include a note that you have received communication from Facebook explaining the purpose of Community Pages and the possibility of future migration, and that you are explicitly requesting that the Community Page be removed. If you do not include that note, you may receive a response from Facebook containing the information above and a requirement to confirm your request so that we can ensure you have all appropriate information before taking a course of action. Please do not respond to this email but follow the instructions above." [Some editing for size and readability – paragraph breaks, etc.]

Flickr

We're open to your suggestions on Flickr beyond the standard SocMed guidance.

Foursquare

We're open to your suggestions on Foursquare beyond the standard SocMed guidance.

Geocaching

1. Bureaus are required to set standards, in writing, for use of Geocaching. Of critical importance is the issue of the geocaching container, the "geocache" itself. Post-9/11, it would be easy for someone unfamiliar with geocaching to become alarmed at finding a box (perhaps an old ammunition can) in a tree or a hole or on a mountainside and to raise an alarm. Instead, we strongly advise that bureau standards include a labeled, transparent box for use as a geocache, complete with an attached explanation of geocaching.

2. Photographs of geocaches must be kept on-file, accompanied by location data (geo-location and "plain English") for convenient cross-referencing, in case of phone calls from law enforcement, Homeland Security or other interested parties.

3. There is no "grandfathering" for established geocaches.

Google Analytics

1. Register a Google account. This account may only be used for services with which DOI has approved TOS and PIA. For example, you may not use it for Gmail or Google Documents at this time.

   Note: Using unauthorized Google products on behalf of DOI is expressly forbidden. Failure to comply may result in disciplinary action. For exceptions to this standard (for example, paying for an enterprise license for Google Maps), contact Interior's Director of New Media.

2. Add Interior.DigitalMedia@gmail.com to your analytics account as a "User" with the User Manager tool.

3. Mask the final octet of all IP addresses. DOI considers a full IP address as PII and there's a strong sense within DOI that we shouldn't be giving Google or any other vendor the ability to track citizen "movement" across government websites, even if that ability isn't used. Google provides instruction on how to mask IP addresses, as do other vendors of similar services.

Here's the code DOI.gov uses for Google Analytics (Note the "_anonymizeIp" item):

```
<script type="text/javascript">
  var _gaq = _gaq || [];
  var pluginUrl = '//www.google-analytics.com/plugins/ga/inpage_linkid.js';
  _gaq.push(['_require', 'inpage_linkid', pluginUrl]);
  _gaq.push(['_setAccount', 'UA-20161686-1']);
  _gaq.push(['_anonymizeIp']);
  _gaq.push(['_trackPageview']);

  (function() {
    var ga = document.createElement('script'); ga.type = 'text/javascript';
ga.async = true;
    ga.src = ('https:' == document.location.protocol ? 'https://ssl' :
'http://www') + '.google-analytics.com/ga.js';
    var s = document.getElementsByTagName('script')[0];
s.parentNode.insertBefore(ga, s);
  })();
</script>
```

Google Maps

1. DOI OCIO no longer purchases DOI-wide licensing for Google Maps. Bureaus may purchase appropriate licenses for Google Maps, while following regular contracting regulations.

2. DOI OCO has completed a general-purpose PIA for WebMaps.

3. For instructions on the use of Google Maps on DOI websites, please consult the documents at: https://portal.doi.net/CIO/ERM/ESC/GoogleMaps/GoogleMapsPremierInstructions_DOI.aspx.

4. Google's Maps API TOS changed Oct. 1, 2011 to include mandatory fees at certain performance levels, as well as the possibility of embedded commercial advertising.

5. We're working to further improve Interior's online map situation. OCO/New Media recognizes the utility of online maps. In the mean time, for static maps, please consider the following alternative: http://www.doi.gov/news/video/Making-a-Map-with-USGS-Seamless-Server.cfm. We have also experimented with taking screenshots of OpenStreetMap maps. We resist the urge to embed live OpenStreetMap maps on DOI websites because we do not wish to burden their .org sites with our traffic.

6. OCIO is working on an alternative to Google Maps which may provide mapping at zero cost to the bureaus. Please contact OCIO for details.

Google Maps Engine Lite / MyMaps

1. MyMaps (formerly GMEL) is now part of Bison Connect.

2. Please feel free to use MyMaps links in email or other short-term products. Who knows what will happen in the long-term?

3. While Google is rebranding and re-integrating the product, the easiest way to get to MyMaps will be to log-in to BisonConnect, then browse over to https://www.google.com/mymaps.

Google Plus

1. When using G+ Hangouts, remember to include live captioning for 508 compliance when appropriate.

2. Public use of a G+ Hangout (a "Hangout on the air") requires captioning.

3. Don't hesitate to share content with communities, after sharing it with the general public.

4. Use images in your posts whenever possible.

5. Beyond the above, we're open to your suggestions on G+ beyond the standard SocMed guidance.

Livestream

1. Within the normal constraints of contracting regulations (including, and not limited to, competition and credit card limits), the Livestream.com video service may be used.

    a. According to the agreed TOS for free Livestream service, advertising will be present, both on your Livestream.com page and as commercial interruptions of the video service. Commercially sponsored official government communication is forbidden except in exigent circumstances.

    b. Ads and commercials are not present on the paid/premium service.

2. 508-Compliance:

    a. For external (public) audiences, live captioning is required.

    b. If live captioning is unavailable, captioned video must be made available after the event.

        i.   Since captioning is readily available on the commercial market, it's unlikely that any non-captioned live video would be authorized. If in doubt, consult with OCO/New Media.

        ii. In the case of breaking news (e.g. an earthquake), live captioning may be unavailable; however, a good-faith attempt to obtain captioning must be made. This would require, at a minimum, making documented requests for captioning service from a regular supplier. OCO/New Media will be happy to share its service providers, but will not require their use. Who you contract with is up to you and your office.

    c. For internal audiences, poll the audience beforehand if possible, to check for the necessity of captioning.

        i.   If captioning is requested, or otherwise known to be required for an audience member or members, then captioning is mandatory.

> ii. If an audience poll has not been conducted, then captioning is mandatory.
>
> iii. If an audience poll has been conducted and no request has been made for captioning, and if it is believed that no audience member requires captioning, then captioning is optional for the live event.

3. The Chat Room:

   a. Livestream chat is authorized, but only in the Livestream or Twitter client, not the Facebook app.

   b. OCO/New Media recommends use of the Livestream chat client, rather than Twitter, because the video-embedding tool only works with Livestream's own chat client.

   c. At the end of a production, the chat-log may be copied by using the usual function keys for your operating system (CTRL-a (all) CTRL-c (copy) on Windows, CMD-a (all) CMD-c (copy) on a Mac). Then paste the chat into a text document (CTRL-v) and save it.

   d. Do not organize archived chat. Chat in a plain text file is not a "system," meaning that a chat log is not a system of records, no matter what its contents are. Drop it into a spreadsheet or database, perhaps organized by the chatters' names, and you've got the potential for a system of records, which might require an amended PIA or SORN.

Before setting-up an account to accommodate an event, check with OCO/New Media, as we may have a timeslot available for your live-streaming event on Livestream.com/Interior.

Pinterest

We're open to your suggestions on Pinterest beyond the standard SocMed guidance.

SlideShare

For all uses of SlideShare, an alternate (.gov) source for public access to the document is required. Don't force the public to submit to .com privacy or other policies in order to obtain government information. Please see **Document- and Data-Sharing Repositories** (above) for general guidance on SlideShare and similar services.

CommonSpot Users

In general, SlideShare is not necessary, as CommonSpot has similar PDF-viewing functionality built-in.

Embedding SlideShare files in .gov Web pages

DOI-sourced documents may be embedded in DOI Web pages using SlideShare, but should be considered a last resort, after failing at providing dot-gov hosting of government documents. Documents must reside on approved DOI SlideShare accounts and be ad-free. DOI OCO pays for an ad-free account. Be certain that rights and permissions for any content are proper for public display. For website users who choose to not use SlideShare, an alternate method of viewing/downloading must be provided. One acceptable alternative would be a 508-compliant downloadable version of the document, with its hyperlink in close proximity (on the next or previous line of text, for example), as here: http://www.doi.gov/news/pressreleases/AMERICAS-GREAT-OUTDOORS-Salazar-Releases-50-State-Report-Highlighting-Projects-to-Promote-Conservation-Outdoor-Recreation.cfm.

Tumblr

We're open to your suggestions on Tumblr beyond the standard SocMed guidance.

Twitter

At present, no online Tweet-management tool (e.g., Hootsuite) except for TwitterFeed (below) is approved for use.

OCO does not vet approvals for desktop software (e.g., Tweetdeck), so reaching out to your CIO shop may be a more fruitful tactic until a SaaS tool is approved.

Official Twitter accounts are the property of the U.S. Department of the Interior. DOI officials should not use their personal accounts for government messaging. Official accounts should not contain the personal names of the Twitter user(s). Official accounts may not be transferred to individuals for personal use. It may be helpful to review this press account (http://www.telegraph.co.uk/news/uknews/9156503/Twitter-storm-hits-Boris-after-he-appropriates-Mayors-official-account.html) for an enhanced understanding of issues we would prefer to avoid with the use of Twitter or other SocMed services.

TwitterFeed

There is some question as to the value of RSS-to-Twitter services, such as TwitterFeed. Robo-feeding your primary Twitter channel is both easy and efficient, but doesn't encourage engagement with any community. However, for an automated jobs feed (e.g., USInteriorJobs), it's ideal. Of course, there's also the question of the value of an automated jobs feed in Twitter.

Wikipedia

1. Abide by Wikipedia's policies and guidelines, also listed under Wikipedia: List of policies and guidelines. Special attention should be paid to the section on content standards. OCO/New Media recommends Wikipedia's "Missing Manual/Introduction" as well.

2. Use of Wikipedia should be preceded by a careful reading of Wikipedia's Five Pillars. Special attention should be paid to the second pillar, "Wikipedia has a neutral point of view."

    a. Verifiable accuracy is a must. Any edit beyond simple copyediting must be accompanied by third-party reference.

    Example (imaginary) 1: A Wikipedia article on geology states that dinosaurs are "mythological beasts which never really existed." USGS public affairs decides to post a correction based on original (but as-yet unpublished) USGS research. This would be a mistake. "Wikipedia articles must not contain original research." It would be better to post the correction based on research published in a peer-reviewed journal. A hyperlink to the peer-reviewed article (or to an article about the peer-reviewed article) would be mandatory (a matter of DOI policy, not Wikipedia's). A government website is not considered as authoritative as a peer-reviewed journal in this context. Since DOI controls DOI websites, DOI websites are not authoritative references for DOI entries in Wikipedia.

Example 2: Administrator X's public affairs guru directs you to change the administrator's Wikipedia page to include the expression "best administrator ever." This would be wrong in several ways, not least of which would be its lack of verifiability. Also, see 3, below, "No puffery."

Example 3: Administrator Y's Wikipedia profile states that she worked for Massive-ish Dynamics prior to her appointment at Interior. The proper company name is Masterful Dynamics. A hyperlink to the company website would be required. A hyperlink to some mention of Administrator Y's work at Masterful Dynamics would be better.

b. Note any changes in the changelog.

c. Any official editing of Wikipedia entries must be done while logged-in using a registered Wikipedia account with a User Page. Any accounts must be named with obvious government/agency identification.

Acceptable Examples: DOI-NewMedia, USGS-Communication, NationalParkServiceOfficial, USInterior, BureauOfReclamationPAO

Unacceptable Examples: Bob, NewMedia, FedGuy, OfficialDude, WebN00b

On occasion, folks ask why we need to be so open about Wikipedia edits, since Wikipedia doesn't require a login. First, the tenets of Open Government require our public actions to be transparent. Second, Wikipedia logs IP addresses and tools such as WikiScanner can track edits back to our agencies and bureaus.

3. No self-aggrandizement. No editing of one's own Wikipedia page. No puffery.

Do not create biography pages.

YouTube

For all uses of YouTube, closed-captioning is required. Don't rely on YouTube's "machine transcription" feature. However, you may use its auto-captioning feature, provided that you provide an accurate transcript. YouTube is much more reliable at timing words to sounds, than it is at determining words from sounds.

Embedding YouTube videos in .gov Web pages

DOI-sourced video files may be embedded in DOI Web pages, but should be considered a last resort, after failing at providing dot-gov hosting of government video. YouTube videos must reside on approved DOI YouTube pages and be ad-free. Be certain that rights and permissions for any content are proper for public performance. **For website users who choose to not use YouTube, an alternate method of viewing must be provided.** One acceptable alternative would be a 508-compliant downloadable version of the video, with its hyperlink in close proximity (on the next or previous line of text, for example).

Note: Using YouTube is trendy in .gov circles, especially for community building. However, DOI continues to warn against relying on a technology platform that requires us to trade citizen privacy for easy distribution of government content. Also, some agencies have noticed that putting videos exclusively on YouTube may prevent those videos from being watched by people at agencies and companies that block YouTube access. Agencies tend to not block other agency websites.

Zoomerang

1. ~~Zoomerang.com's survey service may be used internally, per DOI-wide PIA.~~

2. ~~Zoomerang may also be used externally, provided:~~

    a. ~~You consult with OCO/New Media~~

    b. ~~Your office or bureau conducts a PIA~~

    c. ~~Your office or bureau consults with its appropriate Paperwork Reduction Act specialist. External surveys must generally be approved by OMB. Your PRA specialist should be able to advise you on OMB approval issues. The PRA and OMB approvals are beyond the scope of this document; but in the absence of other guidance, assume that OMB approval is mandatory and schedule accordingly.~~

Zoomerang is now SurveyMonkey. We lack a PIA for SurveyMonkey (See Appendix B).

Appendix B – TOS- (and only TOS-) Approved services

Requirements

The following services have approved is approved Terms of Service for DOI-wide use, however, no DOI-wide PIA has been crafted. Each bureau is required to complete its own PIA and Records work, in order to use these services with a public audience. A lower bar exists for their use with DOI employees (Note Pixlr).

Services

Eventbrite

We're open to your suggestions on Eventbrite beyond the standard SocMed guidance.

SurveyMonkey

We're open to your suggestions on SurveyMonkey beyond the standard SocMed guidance.

Pixlr

Pixlr (the image editing service at Pixlr.com) is winding through our approval process, with every expectation of full approval. Our Solicitor has approved the TOS for image-editing purposes and since our use of Pixlr will not involve providing images to Pixlr for storage or editing, the Privacy Office may be cleared soon. That said, here is our Pixlr guidance:

- Do not create a Pixlr.com account, do not log-in to Pixlr.com, and do not upload any images of human beings to Pixlr.com.

- Feel free to load and edit images in the browser-based image-editor.

Appendix C – Non-Approved services

Requirements

None of the following services is approved for DOI-wide use; however, it's possible that some bureau approval may be in place. In addition, for those awaiting DOI approval, this appendix may serve as a look ahead (a "warning order" to ex-military folks) to what guidance might follow future approval.

1. Remember the TOS/PIA/SORN.

   - **TOS** – DOI must approve terms of service with the provider. GSA approval is not enough.

- **PIA** – DOI requires an approved Privacy Impact Assessment (or preliminary PIA).

- **SORN** – Any social media must be used only within the boundaries of a published System of Records Notice.

2. Request approval from your bureau's social media contact.

   Contact DOI (via GSA's Apps.gov portal, if possible) for all account approvals for services listed in this appendix. One contact person has been assigned responsibility for account management as per negotiation with service providers.

Services

Non-Google Analytics

If possible, mask the final octet of all IP addresses. DOI considers a full IP address as PII and there's a strong sense within DOI that we shouldn't be giving Google or any other vendor the ability to track citizen "movement" across government websites, even if that ability isn't used.

If possible, add newmedia@ios.doi.gov to your analytics account as a "User."

Google products other than those approved

1. Using Google products other than those approved by OCO, OCIO or other proper authority without first obtaining an approved TOS, PIA and (if necessary) SORN is expressly forbidden.

2. Improperly using Google products other than analytics without paying Google or an authorized reseller would compound the situation.

Non-Google Maps

1. DOI OCO has completed a general-purpose PIA for WebMaps; however, we have no approved TOS for any free commercial mapping service.

2. The general-purpose PIA lacks OCIO security approval for any but Google maps. Before implementing a non-Google-map solution, have the solution approved by OCIO.

3. The website language required for Google Maps by the June 23, 2000, memorandum on Google Maps ("Subject: Use of Google Maps Application Programming Interface") is also required for non-Google maps (modified to replace "Google" with the name of the map provider).

4. If, after going through appropriate acquisition processes, your bureau or office decides to use an online mapping solution, contact OCO/New Media for details and proper use under the approved PIA.

3. We're working to improve Interior's online map situation (See 6 above). OCO/New Media also recognizes the utility of online maps. In the mean time, for static maps, please consider the following alternative: http://www.doi.gov/news/video/Making-a-Map-with-USGS-Seamless-Server.cfm.

Appendix C – Response to Social Media Comments

(Adapted from USGS SocMed Response Considerations, adapted from the Air Force Web Posting Response Assessment, Air Force Public Affairs Agency - Emerging Technology Division and Environmental Protection Agency Social Media Response Guidelines.)

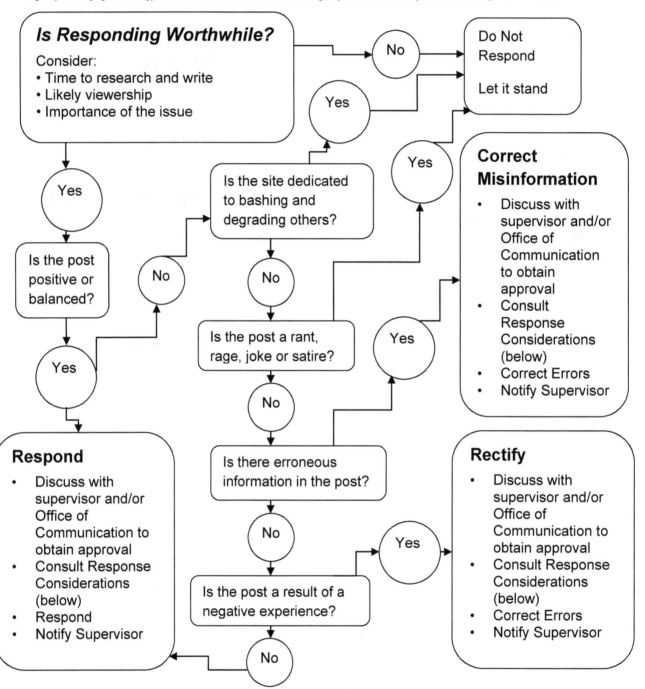

Response Considerations

Be Transparent – Disclose your affiliation (e.g. DOI or contractor).
Cite Your Sources – Stick to facts and cite your sources by including hyperlinks, video, images, etc.
Respect Your Time – Do not spend more time than the response is worth.
Use a Professional Tone – Respond in a tone that reflects positively on Interior.

Unsure of your response, or of how to respond? Contact your Office of Communications for help.